ECHOES OF MIND

SHIVALI KUMARI

To one died star !

I will always keep going , writing and living my life. As I know even though now you are in heaven, but you never wanted me to quit and I know ,

You would never want me to quit ever !

Contents

Contents

Preface

Poetry is the language of the soul, the rhythm of emotions, and the voice that often remains unheard in the noise of life. This book is a collection of verses that capture the essence of human emotions like the fleeting joys, the lingering sorrows, the echoes of longing, and the whispers of hope. Each poem is a reflection of the countless feelings that reside within us, haunting yet comforting, unsettling yet serene.

As human beings, we are destined to feel sometimes with overwhelming intensity, sometimes with quiet acceptance. Our emotions are not just experiences; they are the very essence of our existence. They shape our thoughts, define our relationships, and carve the stories of our lives. This collection is a journey through those emotions and also some light of hope ,Hope very ironic as it keeps us alive but only to kill us at the last ,but it is beautiful with it curse that disturb the heart and also that bring peace to it.

Many of these verses stem from my own emotions, from moments that left imprints on my soul, from voices that echoed in my mind long after they had faded into silence. But I believe these emotions are not just mine they belong to all of us , .We have all loved, lost, hoped, and despaired. We have all felt the weight of memories and the lightness of dreams. These poetic lines will make you , to feel deeply, to reflect, and to embrace the beauty of being human. May these words resonate with you, bring you comfort, or simply remind you that you are not alone in what you feel.

In the end, I hesitate to relate you, dear reader, to these emotions as for to resonate with them means that, at some point in life, you too have been haunted by their presence. And though I do not wish for anyone to carry such burdens.

-Shivali

1. Dear Mumma!

Hey Mumma,
You are strong, a blazing fire,
A soul I endlessly admire.

You are the words my heart longs to speak,
A lesson so precious, one seeks to keep.
Etched in a diary, both fair and true,
A daily wisdom, forever new.

Your words, poetic, a melody divine,
A heroic charm, an endless shine.
Only those beyond the reel
Can feel their depth, so pure, so real.

They strike like stones on castles tall,
Yet lift me up when I might fall.
You are a pearl that always gleams,
Saying, "I'm fine," despite your dreams.

You are my guide, my dearest mate,
Unlocking doors to something great.
When I break and tears descend,
Your presence heals, you help me mend.

A queen without a golden crown,
Always there when I am down.
You bloom like flowers in the spring,
For every child,
Their mother is the wing.

When I gaze into your eyes,
I see a world so beautifully wise.
And I wonder, in my surprise,
Are you an angel in disguise?

You read my silence, my hidden fears,
The pain I mask behind my tears.
Like flowers glow beneath the skies,
You teach love that never dies.

So stay happy, just as you are,
Hiding life's wounds
Like a distant star !

2. Grief (An unwanted guest)

One day,
An unwanted guest came.
I don't remember
When?
Somewhere between admiring
The sorrow of my life,
She entered barefoot
Into my darkened chapel.

Joy was there,
Watching from afar,
Standing in a corner.
But he didn't come,
Perhaps still unsure
If he could carry the weight of my life.

Grief clutched my hand.
She held my tired body
Against hers.
The rain of my tears shattered,
And the cuts on my body found rest—
Almost beautiful!

She didn't question.
She didn't complain.
She wasn't sympathetic.
She didn't say,
"Forget it"
Or "Everything will be okay."
She cherished my scars.

For a moment, I drowned,
Sobbing out my insides.
I stood there,
Like the nakedness of my body,
Clothed with truth,
In her embrace.

She sat with me.
We drank tea.
And the unwanted guest
Became my friend.
I let her win.

And now,
I'm used to that friend !

3. What are we?

In the midst of fortune
And undying hope,
Noble lies wander
Through a beautiful sky.

But suddenly, the truth is uncovered,
And you are left on your own.
You see a naked body,
Covered with the scars of life,
Standing in the mirror—
A person who wishes to die.

Black as a pit,
You survive each day,
Saying, just a little bit.
Neither winced nor cried aloud,
Beyond the place of wrath and tears,
It blooms.

Yet the horror of the shade
Sheerly silences,
Or perhaps your own screaming demons—
But now,

They have become
Your best friends
And sweet lemons.

4. Warmth of nature

I'm exhausted of city life,
Searching for an escape.
The sunshine, ethereal,
Fades my pain a little away.

Long and shady trees,
Peace in the cool breeze,
Butterflies fluttering around,
Birds singing their sounds.

Every moment feels alive,
With music—hymns that soothe.
Majestic and full of colors,
Painted on God's canvas.
A beautiful scent of life lingers.

Even at night,
Though it's a little dark,
The moonglade shines—
Nature's spark all around.

Green meadows stretch everywhere,
Clouds as light as air.

Flowers swaying, their scents abound,
Reminding me of peace and beauty,
Nestled in the lap of these valleys.

The flowing river murmurs,
Its waves whispering to me,
Stories untold.
This beauty wraps around me,
A comforting touch.

From the morning sunrise,
Rising with hope,
"A story to create,"
To evening sunsets,
Ending with a day worth living.

But how can we forget the night?
It holds a glory, a truth,
Inside me, you, and the world around.
In its comforting warmth,
Nature is splendid in every way.

It creates a serene stay,
Where time both continues and pauses,
In the same moment !

5. A poem to my younger self

I'm so proud of you for trying each day,
For doing your best to be okay.
I'm proud of you for waking up,
Even when some yesterday felt too tough.

I know the battles you silently fight,
Without a sword, yet full of might.
I see the weight you carry inside,
But remember,
You were a beautiful art, alive.

You hide so much, deep and wide,
Yet the dark clouds will soon subside.
Sunlight will come, it will be your guide,
Leading you past the storms you survived.

Words can be deceitful, my dear,
So use them wisely, hold them near.
The world won't feel as deeply as you,
But don't let that ever silence you.

A picture is poetry without a sound,

And you, my love, are art unbound.
So Thanku for always smiling
My little cutie pie,
Your heart were vast as the endless sky.

I know what you've been through,
But still you choose to paint
Your life anew.
With colors of your own design,
A masterpiece only you can define.

You don't deserve love that comes in parts,
You deserve a love that fills your heart—
Like a whole pineapple cake, sweet and true,
Overflowing with warmth just for you.

I'm proud of you for being kind and free,
For sometimes acting recklessly,
And for the time
You were mature beyond years,
Even when you hide your silent tears.

I'm proud of you
for embracing new beginnings,
For accepting endings
without proper finishing.
I'm proud of you for breaking free,

And choosing to live with dignity.

I'm proud of you for dressing up for yourself,
For knowing beauty isn't just what's felt.
It's in the soul, in the stars you weave
Through the strands of hair you never leave.

In your ridiculous clothes,
Wrapped in acceptance like a rose,
Telling bad jokes, dancing wild,
A free spirit, a reckless child.

I'm proud of you for enduring pain,
For walking through dark nights in the rain,
For heavy breaths and shivering hands,
Yet still standing, refusing to bend.

You always tried to live the way
You truly desire,
Ignite your soul, set it on fire.
You stayed boldly
Everytime,
I wish I could hug you ,
When you wanted someone to hold ,
wrapped you in their warmth and
Let you pour your inside out
And at last, even if some people

Never treats you right,
Know this-
I love you.

A love that never leaves,
Never reminds, never defines,
Just loves, endlessly,
The way love was meant to be,
The way I and you
We both love !

6. A stranger like fictional

I met a stranger, a man out of a tale,
Holding a Murakami book,
his presence so enchanting,
Handsome as hell or an angel from above,
His eyes held confusion, a trace of being lost.

He asked the owner, Which book is best?
But how can one answer without knowing his quest?
His accent was thick, yet his voice was sweet,
And Murakami's book led our fates to meet.

It started with hello, innocent and kind,
Then drifted to books, where stories unwind.
He let me convince him, with ease and delight,
To read Men Without Women that day ,
I made him fall in love with murakami,
Who wrote epic with pen .

Words swam through the air, a lyrical sea,
Our thoughts like a flood, wild and free.
Drowning in ink, legends came alive,
His voice painting stories, his soul so wise.

He spoke of novels like he had lived their life,
Matured like Kafka, with wisdom innate.
Carrying the scent of old books in his air,
His presence felt timeless, rare and fair.

He told me I could impress anyone with my words alone,
We spoke of authors, not names of our own.
Then time called us back, and we blinked away,
A fleeting moment, yet longing to stay.

Minutes later,
I heard a "hey",
The same sweet voice calling my way.
He held out a book—I said there was no need,
But he insisted,
Just as I had
For Murakami indeed.

We shook hands,
Sealing the day,
No numbers, no names, no words to replay.
Yet our books held the threads of poetic ties,
A silent connection through literary skies.

As he faded, he spoke a line,
A phrase that healed something inside me .

Alluring, unreal, a man from a dream,
Like stars that vanish yet still softly gleam.

We wanted nothing,
No start nor end,
Just two strangers,
With nothing to mend.
But All I want to say is that,
In those world of fleeting and optical stories,
Let's meet again !!

7. When you are dead but not buried

Abandoned by a smile,
As teardrops beg to plead.
Hopeless grief,
In a house of hope,
Built upon a land
Where sorrow storms bleed.

Like a tidal wave,
It pulls me down,
Dragging me deeper, making me drown.
The demons of darkness
Become my friends,
While the real world
Turns its back again.

No one hears my silent screams.
Some days,
I cry inside out,
Other times,
I laugh too much,
Hiding the pain behind a hollow sound.
And sometimes, it's harder

To take that particular shot
The one that shatters all I've got.

Maybe I live in fantasy,
Burying a reality
Too painful to face.
And in this way ,
I end up making
Myself a mystery,
Coiled like a tangled wire,
Desperate to unravel,
To run against the storm's embrace.

But in the end,
Pain knows what I feel.
It knows the real me
Behind the fake painted smiles,
Staying by my side
When even,
I fail to recognize myself.

And that depression
Stays and whispers,
"It's okay,
You'll be better." !

8. The Green bench diaries

A bench painted green, so bright,
Feels like a heart in morning light.
Though simple, still it stands apart,
As in my eyes, it feels like art.
I hear the whispering of the leaves,
A wind's soft lullaby that weaves,
A melody so pure and sweet,
A song where earth and sky both meet.

In golden rays that softly gleam,
The trees beside me cast a dream.
They offer shade in summer's heat,
A gentle place where heartbeats meet.

And when the winter frost draws near,
The little sunrays still appear,
Wrapping me in their embrace,
A fleeting warmth, a soft embrace.

With a cup of hot chocolate near,
I sit in solitude sincere.

No forced smiles, no need for grace,
Just me, my thoughts, my sacred space.

I write the words I'll never speak,
Capturing moments, still and meek.
Like a lens clicks life in view,
This place feels real, this place feels so true.

Like an angel in her space,
With a roaming heart without a trace.
This bench, it holds a part of me,
A quiet love, a memory.

It pulls me in, like hook to eye,
As I sit there, breathing sighs.
And when my friends call me away,
I whisper soft,
A little bye !!

9. The Enigmatic boy

I saw an entity in fields of green,
Where soothing winds wove a tranquil scene.
The day embraced winter's gentle song,
A melody where hearts belong.

Wildflowers swayed with the whispering breeze,
As if nature hummed in silent ease.
And there he stood,
Like autumn's grace,
Moving softly, time slowing its pace.

Yet rain of doubt clung to his name,
A tale unread,
Like full of undecifered history
His eyes, like stars in twilight's hue,
Held secrets vast, and unknown.

He walked with steps so light, so free,
A wandering soul—
Lost, yet seen.
Wanting shadows, craving light,
Standing still, yet shining bright.

His smile, divine yet veiled in ache,
His lips said "fine,"
Hough hearts could break.
A man full of ironies,
Or echoes of agonies
Standing silently but presence so loud,
A silent sorrow in laughter bold.

He danced beneath the sunbeam's glow,
A vision dark, yet bathed in gold.
And though I knew him not at all,
My soul still heard his silent call.

So I begged the universe, soft and low,
"Let me heal this wandering soul."
Even if plenty of knives
Still pierce my back,
Even if fate won't grant me that.

Perhaps one day, I'll truly know,
Or maybe, I never will
As for now , I don't know!!

10. Scars that speak

Do my scars frighten you?
Do they whisper of my past?
Do they scream stories long buried
In an unnamed grave,
Somewhere in the silence of the night?

Yet, even graves have whispers,
Echoes of what once was.
And my scars ,faint as they seem but
Still carry the weight of those hushed confessions.

But let me tell you otherwise
What I am
Is the aftermath of all I was.
These scars bled in the past,
Yet now, they have faded into echoes.

The depths I once drowned in,
Now you feel when you read me.
I have walked far from the pain,
Yet, somehow,
I remain trapped in its shadow.

What once tore me apart
Is now history, engraved upon my body,
Reflected in my eyes,
Etched into my words.

Once, I was a woman of silence,
Now, I hold stories worth telling.
I built myself back,
Resurrected from the grave
Where I had once been laid to rest.

The only sad part is that
I died that day ,
Yet the scars live on,
Reminders of a past I no longer claim.

Who was I then, years ago?
Perhaps just a fleeting face,
A forgotten name,
A shadow erased by time.
And so,
You all will erase too

Both this (me) and that,

Vanishing into the

Unnamed grave by unknown name !

11. Social confessions

What's in my wallet?
What's on my feet?
The brand of my jacket,
The food that I eat.

My eyes are here,
Yet you never meet them
Instead, you stare at my bracelets,
You admire my diamonds,
But never see my demons.

Is there a bridge to close this gap,
Between what I have and what I lack?
Between what I show and what I hide,
Between the truth and the polished lies?

The world is there ,
But a fleeting shadow,
While everyone chases dead stars,
Blindly running toward illusions,
Forgetting who they truly are.

Hey, look into my eyes,

Feel what I feel.
Let the day slip by unnoticed,
Forget the bills, forget the deals.

You are a vortex of unsaid words,
A soul yearning for confession,
Not a name bound by price tags,
Not a life shaped by possessions.

Strip away the glittering noise,
Let's speak in truths, not trends.
For what matters isn't what we wear,
Scared of known or remain unknown
What is your fear ?

12. Somewhere in multiverse

Somewhere in the multiverse,
There is a little girl
Lies in a field of flowers,
Playing with Her long Rapunzel hair
Spilling like golden threads,
As butterflies waltz upon her cheeks,
And fireflies hum lullabies
Into the twilight air.

The sun kisses her face,
And the burn from the sun
Is the most painful thing she ever feels
She dwells in a garden,
Where a quaint cottage stands,
A home where,
Wolves roam as gentle friends.
For she has learned,
"The wolves must be gentler than any man"

She writes in journals,
ink-stained and free,
For paper holds more patience

Than any soul she's ever met.
She reads ; oh, how she reads!
Plato and Austen,
Socrates and Shakespeare,
Freud and Sylvia, lost in their worlds.
No semesters binds her,
No syllabus contains her,
For she has built her own library,
Not gifted by A beast to A beauty,
But crafted by her own hands,
Her own dreams.

Sometimes, she dances,
To slow jazz under the moon's silver glow,
Belle-like twirls or contemporary grace,
Never chasing perfection,
Only feeling the music.
And sometimes,
She finds herself in a slow dance,
With a man ,
Who stumbles through the rhythm,
Yet matches the intimacy in her gaze,
And the silence between their breaths.

And when the cottage walls feel too small,
They venture beyond ,
Side by side,

Beneath the northern lights,

Sipping tea together .

As the universe,

Spins its infinite tales around them !

13. Is it truly beautiful?

Is it love, or is something concealed?
Are hidden truths silently repealed?
Is there pain that leaves no scars,
Or does beauty fade when seen from afar?

Do their steps dance with love's embrace,
Or does unseen force dictate their pace?
Is this truly a pure symphony,
Or is something veiled behind sweet honey?

Is it destiny, written in fate,
Or are there stories carved with hate?
Is all we see the honest truth,
Or merely what they choose as proof?

Is it pleasure, soft and sweet,
Or something silenced, forced, discreet?
Is it truly something lovely,
Or tangled truths wrapped subtly?

Is it an eternal work of art,
Or a canvas stained with bleeding hearts?
Is it a flower in full bloom,

Or whispers lost in silent gloom?

Are these butterflies that softly soar,
Or masks concealing something more?
Is it perfect, as it seems,
Or perfectly flawed within its seams?

Not bound by person, place, or name,
But questioning all that beauty claims,
Is it truly flawless, pure, and bright,
Or merely shadows dressed in light?

14. Moon and you

Two words, meant love .
The moon in tainted, lovely skies,
And you, with those tangerine eyes.
Both, like museums full of art,
Where I wander lost,
Leaving all the things apart.

You and the moon
A living fairytale, a celestial grace,
A beauty so eternal, time cannot erase.
You make me believe in fate's gentle design,
And dream of a reality where you are mine.

Even the slightest glance is enchantment,
Your presence,
a warmth that thaws
The coldest heart.
I cherish you and the moon's quiet glow,
As if they were pieces of my very soul.

Every moment feels divine,
And watching you is finer than any wine.
A radiant aura, a soft golden hue,

Brightening my days
With love pure and true.

This love, an endless symphony,
A melody echoing through eternity.
It carves light into my darkest nights,
Filling my world with colors bright.

Yet, like the moon,
I admire you from afar.
A celestial beauty I cannot grasp.
My eyes hold you in an unbreakable gaze,
A love etched in time,
Through endless days.

Even if love fades into mere words,
Even if distance turns it unheard,
I can never forget
The warmth you make me feel
Like the moon, forever in my dreams.

For every phase, every silver gleam,
You are my moon, my timeless theme.
A selenophile at heart, I vow to stay,
Loving you like the moon, in every way !

15. Listening through the silences

Silence speaks louder
Than any words ever could.
I hear the hush between sentences,
A truth untouched by sound.
The stillness of an inhale
Does it whisper a life fulfilled,
Or swallow a lie unspoken?

I listen to silence as it echoes,
Carrying the chaos hidden
That is hidden behind your
Enchanting laughter,
Silence of people 's pauses
The pauses in conversation,
Weighted with untold stories
That is more than paragraphs
Deeper than a thousand words.

The quiet envelope of a soul,
You think no one notices,
But I do. I read it too.
It is tragic and ironic,

How your silent thoughts scream,
Yet no one seems to hear.

Is the world deaf,
Or do there is any bounce of walls,
Timeless words linger in the air
As strangers pass me by,
Their soft lips, their shining eyes
Revealing silences of love, fear,
Desire, sorrow
Unheard voices of the soul.

But what of the silence within me?
When the quiet becomes haunting,
Hiding in the ticking clock,
The rattling fan, the humming air
Wrapping itself around me,
Peering into my naked soul.

I fear these silences.
The silence of being ignored by one
The silence of beautiful lies,
The silence in trembling, broken stories,
The silence of buried thoughts,
The silence left by nightmares.

And then ,
I crave words.
Though I know silence holds truth,
Somewhere deep within me
But I still find it deceptive.

In the end, I wonder
Does silence reveal the truth,
Or does it merely conceal it?
At last I don't know !

16. Promise of Falling leaves

It was autumn
The season of sadness,
Where sadness lingers in the crisp air,
And truths once hidden in summer's glow
Now stand bare, like an unclothed soul.

On an aging tree, two leaves remained,
Side by side, through seasons untamed.
From the bloom of spring's gentle embrace
To summer's blaze and the weeping rain,
They clung to each other, steadfast and true.

But now, the time had come,
The season of falling had arrived.
And more than the fear of withering,
They trembled ,
At the thought of parting ways.

The first leaf whispered,
"Can it be… that we meet again,
On the ground below,
And in each other's embrace,

Endure the coldness of winter?"

The second leaf, soft in its sorrow, replied,
"Yes, perhaps, if fate allows,
If we fall together,
At the same time, in the same place."

"But what if we don't?" the first leaf quivered.
"What if we fall apart,
Carried by different winds,
Scattered across unknown lands?
What if I never find you again?
What if you forget my existence?"

A silence settled,
Then the second leaf spoke,
Yes, it may happen,
That we never meet again in this world.
But I promise you ,
It can never happen
That I forget you.

Even in the coldest of winters,
When the earth is draped in frost,
I will warm myself with the memory of you.
Your presence, your touch,
Will never fade from me."

The first leaf sighed,
A promise forming in the rustling wind.
"Then I promise you this
Even in another world,
I will find you.
And I will never let you
Bear the cold alone."

And so, in the breath of autumn's final whisper,
They fell,together yet apart,
Carrying their promises into the unknown.

But tell me, dear reader,
Do you think they met again
In that world beyond the fall?

17. The shadows of fear

We are all afraid,
Entangled in shadows we cannot escape.
Fear plays its little game of hide and seek,
Lurking in corners, waiting to halt our steps
Or teaching us to run swifter than the wind.

Sometimes, we outrun it,
Stealing fleeting moments of joy,
But other times, it engulfs us whole,
Locking us in a cage woven with worry.

But what truly unsettles you?
What is it that grips your soul so tight?
Is it the merciless gaze of society,
Or the pitiful stares that strip you bare?
Do you fear death's cold embrace,
Or the aching emptiness of an unlived life?

Are you terrified of fearless storms,
Or the silence that lingers after they pass?
Do you dread the comfort of a lie,
Or the weight of the truth hidden beneath?

Is it the darkness that unsettles you,
Or the visions it unveils within?
Are you afraid of being unseen,
Or petrified of being truly known
Exposed, vulnerable, raw?

You say you fear love,
Or is it the agony of love unreturned?
You dread failure,
Or is it the truth of where you fell short?

In truth, it is not the world you fear,
But the echoes of your own mind
The illusions you weave,
Terrified they may become real.

And so, afraid of drowning,
You never step into the ocean.
But tell me,
Is a life untouched by the waves ?
A life truly lived at all?

18. A night owl's lament

I'm a night owl, wide awake,
Lost in the cold as the hours break.
Where even the breath of the night I hear,
In the restless wind of the intales.

The dark sky stretches, vast and wide,
And in its depths, my joys collide.
When I see the brightest star,
I feel the presence from afar—
Of someone who became a memory,
Yet lingers still, a part of me.

The silence hums a melody sweet,
As night and I in solace meet.
I wander deep through endless thought,
To places ,
No one else consciousness has sought.

There, I am whole,
Not complaining in a tarnished and worn
There, I find new dreams reborn.
In quiet whispers, I wonder, I pray,
To unburden the weight I bear each day.

But alas !
This road is steep,
Each step forward—like rain so deep.
My heart clings tight, afraid to release,
It says mind 'you don't know '
Yet my mind pleads,
"Let it be peace, it's time to let go "

I feel like a ship, adrift, alone,
Lost in its own master ocean
Which is vast and wild,
Seeking a beacon, soft and mild.

Yet chains of the past still pull me tight,
By Holding me hands
And Old wounds stay rent free
Though scars maybe won't show,
But those ,
Echoes of pain that refuse to go.

How long have I been haunted ?
By someone living,
The fear of the unknown grips me tight,
Yet hope still flickers, soft and bright.

And every night, with silent pleas,
I whisper softly—"Release me."
Let's escape, let's take a flight,
To somewhere in a golden light !!

19. What's beauty?

The Beauty in Imperfection

I wonder why?
Perfection draws attention,
Where do your eyes wander?
A flawless face , a picture pristine
A bloom untouched
What is your idea of perfection?
Whom do you call beautiful?

Is there a measure, a rule, a scale?
Or any criteria of beauty?
And if there is, then who decreed it so?
If beauty truly lies ,
Within the beholder's gaze,
Then why is one mocked or bullied
For being "ugly" ?
While another is adored for being "pretty"?

I think , "Pretty"
This word is a lie.
A six-letter illusion spun with fragile threads:
Lose weight, clear fair skin,

Chose colour of your eyes,
And something called ideal height!

If this all define 'beauty',
Then it is a mere reflection,
Not perfection.
For people are not paintings, not statues,
Not sculpted by the hands of expectation.
They are real only in their imperfections.

The little flaws that make you
"you",
The wrinkles that map the years you've lived,
The scars that whisper untold stories,
The tear-stained eyes, the unguarded laughter,
The tangled hair, the freckled skin
Every mark a testament of existence,
Not a flaw, but a signature of self.

So do not shrink into shadows,
No need to hide the pieces
You fear they'll despise.
For it is in these unpolished edges,

In the raw, unfiltered truth of you,
That beauty breathes,
That this is also beauty!!

20. I'm tired!

I'm tired.
Tired of life, of myself,
Or perhaps of the people around me.
I don't know, but I am tired.

I'm too tired to even grab a pen
And write down my thoughts,
As if starting over is something sacred,
Something too heavy to touch.

I'm so tired, yet I cannot sleep.
Something keeps pushing me down,
Pulling me deeper into the abyss.
My mind screams aloud,
But the only sound is silence.

I am too tired to pretend anymore,
Too tired to say that I'm okay
When deep inside,
Nothing is okay.

I'm tired of being hurt by everyone,
Tired to the point where I can't handle anything anymore.

Living alone is terrifying,
But it's the only thing my heart can afford.

I'm so tired of feeling everyone else's pain
That my own has become meaningless.
I feel like a hollow shell,
A corpse unable to express emotion,
Just carrying hurt deep within.

And I'm scared,
Scared I'll never be whole again.

I'm tired of wiping my tears,
So much so that I don't cry anymore.
A version of me had died ,
A long before
And I better know that ,
It will never return !!

21. A girl like no other

A girl with short hair,
Shallow yet daring in her stare.
She was never like folklore,
But she dances freely on the shore.

Not a princess of the world,
But a warrior in her own kingdom.
Haunted by dark nightmares,
Yet she lives as if she doesn't care.

Her smile is beautiful,
A veil to hide the pain.
She gathers courage to walk,
Even when all her strength is drained.

She longs for a place to call home,
But in the end,
All she finds is a girl in the mirror,
Whispering her own sweet name.

Caught between emotions and dark illusions,
Yet she lives her life
Like a sky painted with rainbow hues.

A mixture of joy and sorrow,
But grateful to hear that
Those are the things,
She had not borrow.

A girl with sweet dreams,
Her tears sound like raindrops,
Yet they shine like flames.
She keeps her feelings locked away,
Like a silent, unyielding rock.

She is both vulnerable and free,
Not a fairytale girl who doesn't exist,
But one who fights
Even after the scars on her wrists.

So live life by being
In darkest of nights,
Yet shine like the brightest star.
And love yourself,
Just the way you are !

22. Memories

Do Memories Last Forever?

Even if they fade
In the smoke of time,
Yet they remain imprinted,
Like an unknown grave,
It's dead but still there,
Lost in the mysteries of time.

For me,
Memories are home.
People leave,
Things are abandoned,
Places are destroyed,
Yet memories remain.

There was a time
They existed,
And I was there too.

Desperately,
I hold them again .
Yet sometimes,

I wish to let them go.
Memories can haunt,
Painful, broken,
Leaving me searching for all the "whys".

I recall them
Sometimes through my smile,
And sometimes
Through the salty taste of my tears.

Yet, I hope never to forget,
As they hold my story.
Even when my eyes never stay dry,
I can hold some souls
In my arms once again,
A reminder
That they are with me,
In my memories,
Always !!

23. Breathe of dying star!

There was a star,
One that never wished to fade,
That longed to shine forever,
Defying the night, the rage, the abyss.
A star tougher than stone,
Yet more fragile than a flower's petal.

But one day,
A stone settled upon its chest
And then another, and another,
Pressing against ribs
That refused to break,
Suffocating but never
Shattering Or killing .

The weight grew heavier,
Not crushing, not killing,
But rotting, festering,
Turning something radiant
Into something unrecognizable,
A beauty lost in the torment of longing.

Still, the star endured,
Carrying the burden alone,
Whispering into the endless void,
"Release me… I want to live."
Hoping, praying,
That perhaps
The universe might echos back.
But the silence swallowed every plea.

It called for help too
And the world listened,
Heard the tremors in its voice,
Felt the agony in its glow,
Yet no hands reached out
To share the weight of the stones.

So, in time,
The star came to understand that
This is unbearable,
This is the end.
If freedom meant destruction,
Then let it be so.

And with a final breath,
It collided with the burden it bore,
A supernova exploding into the night,
A magnificent death,

A final act of defiance.

Now, no light remains,
No warmth, no glow
Now there is no star
That shines,
It's Only a black hole,
That exists.
A silent void where a star once shine
Swallowed everything ,
Even the echoes of its own cries ...!

24. The Weight of "Sorry"

You say you're sorry,
But I won't say it's fine,
As no apology can turn back time.
A word so simple, a sound so small,
Yet it can't undo the weight of it all.

A five-letter word cannot mend the scars,
Nor heal the wounds that have bled too far.
Trust, once shattered, turns into dust,
And "sorry" crumbles under the weight of the unjust.

Saying "sorry" is easy—just lips and air,
But to forgive? That's a burden unfair.
For words alone can never restore
What is lost, what is broken,
What exists no more.

I've seen "sorry"
Tossed like a passing phrase,
Used to erase but not to replace.
People speak it, then turn away,
Never meaning the things they say.

For wounds aren't healed by empty lines,
Nor do echoes of regret realign
The bridges burned, the hearts betrayed,
Some things are lost, some debts unpaid.

So keep your sorry, don't let it spill,
Unless it comes with a heart that's still.
Still in remorse, still seeking to mend,
Not just a word, but a vow to amend.

For "sorry" should never be just a sound,
But a promise to build
Where trust broke down.
And until it holds the weight of truth,
It will just remain
" An empty excuse".... !

25. The quiet curse of poet

Being a poet is a quiet curse,
Where words cling like shadows,
Dense and perverse.
They pull you deep into endless thought,
A prisoner of meanings you never sought.

You turn your pain into something divine,
Carving beauty from sorrow, line by line.
Yet, in the end, you're left alone,
Bleeding for verses no one will own.

Ink stains paper like wounds that weep,
Yet your lines are whispers
The world won't keep.
Sometimes,
You wish your mind were still,
That thoughts would fade instead of fill.

They call you wise, as if you know,
But inside,
You're lost where meaning won't grow.
Drowning beneath the weight of words,

Seeking truths that remain unheard.

Most words fall like withered leaves,
Forgotten before they touch the breeze.
Yet, you write,
Because silence is worse,
An emptiness that feels like a curse.

Here, on paper, you finally stand,
Accepting the hollow
In both worlds at hand.
Inside, outside ; alone, yet whole,
No cries for help, no pleading soul.

No complaints, no hatred in return,
Just quiet acceptance as the pages burn.
Tears and ink merge, dark and deep,
A poet's blood ,sacrificed to keep ?

Jab log chale jaate hai toh
Unki yaadein aur Aadatein ko
kaha dafnaati ho ?
"Apni kavityaaon mein shayad ,, !

www.ingramcontent.com/pod-product-compliance
Lightning Source LLC
Chambersburg PA
CBHW031331130726
47988CB00007B/3093